IMAGES
of America

THE DORY FLEET
OF PACIFIC CITY

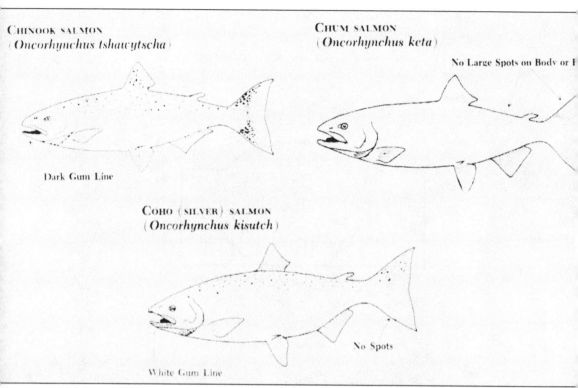

CHINOOK SALMON
(*Oncorhynchus tshawytscha*)

Dark Gum Line

CHUM SALMON
(*Oncorhynchus keta*)

No Large Spots on Body or F

COHO (SILVER) SALMON
(*Oncorhynchus kisutch*)

No Spots

White Gum Line

Ah, the salmon. Oh, how we love thee and want to catch thee. Salmon are considered a game fish and therefore must be caught with a line and a hook. This was not always the case. Before House Bill 282 passed in 1927, fishermen were allowed to catch salmon in the Nestucca River with gill nets or drift nets, whichever they preferred to use. The 1927 bill not only denied them the use of nets, it flat-out denied them the use of the Nestucca River for commercial fishing. Local farmers and dairymen who had been using the commercial fishing industry to supplement their incomes were now left to flounder.

ON THE COVER: Nicknamed for his red hair, "Brick" Gilman (right) was one of the pioneers of the Pacific City Dory Fleet. Dories are built with spruce plank, and as one can see, the early dories were not very big. In this view, Haystack Rock is to the left and Cape Kiwanda to the right. (Courtesy Oregon State Archives.)

IMAGES
of America

THE DORY FLEET
OF PACIFIC CITY

Jeanna Rosenbalm Bottenberg

ARCADIA
PUBLISHING

Published by Arcadia Publishing
Charleston, South Carolina

Library of Congress Catalog Card Number: 2007940252

For all general information contact Arcadia Publishing at:
Telephone 843-853-2070
Fax 843-853-0044
E-mail sales@arcadiapublishing.com
For customer service and orders:
Toll-Free 1-888-313-2665

Visit us on the Internet at www.arcadiapublishing.com

This book is for my dad, Ken Rosenbalm.
In my heart, you are always fishing.

And for all dorymen, past, present, and future. May I honor you.

CONTENTS

ACKNOWLEDGMENTS

There are several people without whom this book would not have occurred. Terry Learned, I cannot begin to say what your kindness and knowledge has meant to me. T. Larkins, your images and stories are great. Ginny Jacobs allowed me to honor her brother, the late Bob Hill, by sharing his spectacular photographs. My family has been amazing, from throwing out ideas to babysitting. Dad, thanks for letting me call in the middle of the night and for providing your support. Ian, I want to thank you for being patient with Mommy while she has been tied up at the computer. I am also grateful to Julie Albright, my editor at Arcadia Publishing. Julie, you have been fabulous and extremely tolerant with this first-time author. And Ray, you are amazing.

Other folks who helped out and to whom I give my most grateful thanks are as follows: Rob Kliever; Walt Miller; Stan and Roseanne Goffena; Mike and Kathy Dixon; Lloyd and Marilyn Rosenbalm; Genevieve Brutke; Daryn and Janell Brutke; Charles Summers; Paul Hanneman; Craig Wenrick; the late Alice Learned; the entire Learned family; the Tillamook County Pioneer Museum; the Tillamook County Libraries in Tillamook and Pacific City; Dave Wendell, Todd Shaffer, and Tim Backer of the Oregon State Archives; and Pat Solomon and Greg Westergaard of the Oregon Department of Transportation. If I have forgotten anyone, I am truly sorry. I have appreciated every bit of help I have received on this journey.

INTRODUCTION

The history of the Pacific City Dory Fleet spans nearly 100 years and serves as an example of the power of the human spirit and the resilience of man in the face of adversity. The Pacific City Dory Fleet has held a place in my heart, even though I have not always known just how special this little group of boats is.

The area around Pacific City and Woods originally was populated with farmers and dairymen for the most part, and these early pioneers found that selling fish commercially provided an added boost to their meager incomes. A 1908 census lists only eight folks as full-time fishermen. Most commercial fishermen found the waters of the Nestucca plentiful enough for their needs and fished using gill nets or drift nets. Gill nets are designed so that fish swim into them up to their gills and the gills get caught in the netting. These stationary nets are placed in the path of spawning salmon. Drift nets work on basically the same principle except they are not fixed; they glide.

A small salmon cannery operated near the mouth of the Nestucca River for some 40 years but finally closed for good in 1926. In January 1927, two representatives from District 13 in McMinnville, Arthur McPhillips and Walter Russell, introduced House Bill 282, which effectively shut down the Nestucca River for commercial fishing. In a whirlwind of legislation, the bill passed through the House and the Senate and was signed into law in February. Why would they want to do this? What do legislators from the valley care what the commercial fishermen on the coast are doing?

The Nestucca River was a sport fishermen's paradise. Loaded with fish, it was also the most easily accessible to anglers from the Willamette Valley. Nestucca sport fishermen felt the nets threatened their ability to catch wild salmon on the random trips they made to the river. There were other, more hidden agendas as well, and all of the reasons seem to be self-serving at best, but I am biased. In the end, some 80 fishermen were displaced, but they went out swinging. Landowners along the river began posting "No Trespassing" signs and having valley anglers arrested for being on their property. Opponents immediately introduced a referendum to House Bill 282 and sought to have the bill overturned. Those in support of the bill chose not to fight their battle in the voter's pamphlet, however, and enlisted the media instead, launching a full-scale assault on coastal commercial fishermen. It proved the most effective method of attack, and when the referendum went to the people for a vote in June 1927, the effort to reopen the Nestucca River failed.

Down but not out, the local fishermen pulled a few tricks out of their hats. Some tried fishing the waters of other coastal rivers, as only the Nestucca had been targeted for closure. These other rivers were not the waters they knew, and they were not able to bring in the catch they had previously. Others fished the Nestucca under cover of darkness, risking fines and imprisonment. Some even recall being shot at as they tried to escape capture. Ultimately, though, these fishermen ended up in the ocean, adapting to the new law of the land.

Dories have been used on the ocean since about 1910. The first brave souls to venture onto the open sea used oars and sails to get around and typically entered by rowing through the treacherous waters at the mouth of the Nestucca River, named after the local Nestugga Indian tribe. The fishermen soon figured out that launching and landing through the surf was safer than the churning water where river met ocean and that the harbor they already had was protected from the prevailing northwest winds and swells, making it the perfect location for dory fishing. At this point, the fleet numbered between 5 and 10 boats.

In the 1930s, inboard motors were introduced, allowing dorymen to motor around in the open ocean, but they still rowed out and in through the surf. Commercial outrigger poles were added, as well as gurdies, to replace the hand-over-hand method of pulling lines. These poles allowed more lines to be cast off of the boat. Early fishing lines only ran about 4 spreads from their poles, but fishermen today have been able to increase that number to 10 or 12 off each line. With two tips and two deeps, it amounts to over 40 lines in the water, greatly increasing the odds of catching a fish. Should the springs bounce and the bell tinkle, though, each one of those lines has to be checked to find the fish. Once the fish is landed, the spread has to be reset and all of the lines put back in the water.

The next improvements to come along were the "gurdies," which are spools of wire that can be dropped deeper than hand lines. Found at an army surplus store in Portland, the gurdies were brought back to the fishermen at Pacific City. Now instead of pulling in their lines, the fishermen were able to reel them in. As the use of gurdies increased, "spreads" (the actual fishing lines) changed, along with how they were made. Woven cotton gave way to stainless steel, and Oregon Green twine gave way to "snubbers," or pieces of stretchy rubber that allow the spread some give so that it is less likely to snap when a fish strikes, and synthetic fishing line. Spreads could now be removed as they were brought up, decreasing the likelihood of a tangle. The military had used the gurdies to catch radio signals on their airplanes, and now the dorymen would use them to catch fish from their boats. These original hand-crank gurdies would eventually be replaced by the new and improved hydraulic gurdies, run by a small hydraulic pump attached to the boat motor.

The dory boat itself has also gone through a transformation. The original boats were much smaller than the modern versions—only about 16 feet in length. They had very little freeboard (the amount of siding left above the water line), sometimes just 22 inches or so. The early boats also had more flare to the sides and a bit of a curve to the bottom. In the 1950s, the square stern was introduced to the fishermen of the Pacific City Dory Fleet. Although initially skeptical, they soon recognized the benefits of this modification and so began building their boats in this manner instead of the two pointed ends.

The traditional double-ender now became a hybrid skiff. The square stern allowed outboard motors to be attached to the back of the boat, soon completely changing the way dorymen accessed the waters of the Pacific. Instead of rowing through the surf, they were now able to motor through it. They could also motor through the surf on the way in and slide up on shore, as many have witnessed. The square-stern construction increased the space in the boat, and soon fish trays and fish boxes were added. Now fishermen reeling in their gurdy lines had somewhere to lay the spread as it was brought up. Some guys were so good they could crank the gurdy with their left hand and lay out the spreads with their right, or vice versa, depending on which side of the boat they were on. With all these new additions, dories were becoming longer and heavier. The average dory today spans 22 feet and weighs approximately 3,000 pounds when fully equipped.

As dory fishing evolved, more and more folks became interested in the sport. The rag-tag little fleet of 10 or so grew to more than 300 during the heyday of commercial fishing. The late 1970s and early 1980s were a boom time for the fleet. Trailers would line up two and three deep on the beach, and fishermen could make over $1,000 a day. Soon, though, governmental restrictions limiting the fishing season and prohibiting new fishing licenses, along with other skullduggery, began to take its toll. The 1984 commercial season was eliminated altogether. Russian and Japanese mega-trollers were scooping up fish by the thousands, and the Pacific City Dory Fleet was fighting to stay afloat. The 1980s were a hard time for the fishermen, as well as ancillary industries, such as the Kiwanda Fish Company. Other local businesses had to close. Restaurants that had served these fishermen through the glory years were now scraping to get by.

Even as the fishing industry declined, tourism flourished. Surfers had long found the beach at Cape Kiwanda a nice place to practice their craft, but the 1990s saw a huge increase in the amount of people who preferred this little, unknown section of beach to other options, such as Lincoln City, Newport, and Seaside. While the number of tourists grew, the number of fishermen shrank, and as often happens, the needs of the many outweighed the needs of the few. The Kiwanda Fish Company is now an RV park. The Hungry Harbor Restaurant (named after the Hungry Harbor, near the mouth of the Nestucca River) now operates as a hotel. The little pizza joint and miniature golf course that we loved as kids is gone, replaced by the Pelican Brew Pub. The Sunset West Café, where untold numbers of fishermen started their days (and where many of my childhood memories lie), is now a parking lot. The dune where we ran back and forth, sat and watched boats come in all summer, and planted our lawn chairs for the Fourth of July fireworks is now off limits, with access restricted to only those who have purchased one of the timeshare condominiums that now hover over the beach.

I would be lying if I said that all of this "progress" does not make me sad or angry. It is difficult to watch memories be torn down and paved over. I know the development is inevitable, but that does not make it any easier to swallow. There is a plus side to all of this: renewed interest in the dory fleet. The owners of the condominiums have worked with the Pacific City Dorymen's Association to improve the access ramp to the beach, originally installed in 1978. They are also erecting a memorial wall in honor of the dory fleet and the dorymen themselves. A list of dory names will grace this memorial wall, along with a bronze statue.

The future of the dory fleet is unknown. Current administration at the state level would like to see marine reserves along the Oregon Coast, already heavily restricted and regulated. These marine reserves could end commercial fishing off of Cape Kiwanda entirely, bringing to a close 100 years of tradition and honor.

One

A SNAPSHOT OF THE DORY FLEET

Through necessity and perseverance, the Pacific City Dory Fleet has evolved into what we see today. The shape of the boat has changed from that of a traditional dory, with two pointed ends, to the modern square-stern variety. Fishing lines have transitioned from woven cotton pulled hand over hand to stainless-steel wires pulled hydraulically. The first gurdies, purchased from World War II surplus, had originally been used to reel in radio antennae that were being pulled behind airplanes. This inexpensive equipment made the job of pulling lines much easier.

The first dorymen hauled their boats to the cape with horse-drawn wagons, and then left them on the beach after the long trek through the sand from the access near Pacific City. The boats were either carried to the water or rolled down on logs or barrels. Roads came, as did vandals, so the boats then had to be hauled back and forth each day. The traditional design of the trailer was modified by local service station owner Paul Hill. He built trailers that could tilt, easing the jobs of dumping and loading the boats.

This chapter will be but a brief glimpse at this amazing handful of boats and some of the changes endured.

Fishing is nothing new to Cape Kiwanda. As evidenced by this early-1900s view, fishermen regularly journeyed to the water's edge for a taste of ocean-caught fish. They are standing on the rocks that dot the southern side of Cape Kiwanda. (Courtesy Tillamook County Pioneer Museum.)

This photograph shows an early Oregon salmon cannery. The Nestucca River played host to a salmon cannery for some 40 years. Four different companies tried to make a go of it—and did, until 1926. In 1927, the Nestucca River was closed to commercial fishing.

Prior to 1927, the ocean was not the main source of commercially caught fish. Local farmers, dairymen, and tradesmen wishing to supplement their income found an ample supply of salmon in the nearby Nestucca River. It was not necessary to brave the waters of the ocean, although some did. Most fishermen cast their nets in the river and pulled in scores of fish. (Courtesy Tillamook County Pioneer Museum.)

These folks appear to be on a pleasure cruise, as they are casting no lines, only their eyes on the beautiful scenery. The Pacific is renowned for its stunning coastline, and the view is even better from the water. It is a view that probably very few had seen when this photograph was taken at the start of the 20th century. (Courtesy Tillamook County Pioneer Museum.)

Barely one month into office, Republican governor I. L. Patterson signed House Bill 282 into law on February 26, 1927, banning commercial fishing in the Nestucca River. A hard-fought battle for repeal was waged by representatives from coastal districts, but on June 28, 1927, the citizens of Oregon voted to uphold the law. (Courtesy Tillamook County Pioneer Museum.)

Local fishermen continued to fish the Nestucca River, although very much on the sly. They cast and pulled their nets at night. During the day, they created huge diversions to distract officials so they could then pull their nets. They posted sentries and covered one another's backs. But eventually they ended up on the ocean. One early member of this elite club of fishermen was Vic Learned Jr. He is pictured here about 1946 with his spruce-planked double-ender. In this photograph, the boat is black, but later in the 1940s it was painted white with red trim. Following that, either side of the stern was decorated with an image of cartoon character Snuffy Smith and the name of the boat, *Shifless Skonk*. Vic's son Terry Learned remembers that the boat always leaked. (Courtesy Alice Learned.)

In the early years of dory fishing, fishermen wheeled their boats up the beach from the access near the present location of Pacific City's bridge. Once in the shelter of Cape Kiwanda, they simply left their boats there for the duration of the season. There was no real worry of theft or vandalism. (Courtesy Bob Hill.)

Paul Hill designed and built a tilting boat trailer in the early 1960s. Dorymen could now just back up into the surf and dump their boats. As the tow rig is gunned forward, the trailer tilts and the boat slides off along the rollers, splashing into a foot or so of water. Hill built about 50 of these trailers for local fishermen. (Courtesy Bob Hill.)

With the construction of roads and bridges and increasing numbers of fishermen, boats began to be hauled back and forth. Paul Hill never fished, but he built trailers and repaired engines. Hill and his son Lee also built this dune buggy, nicknamed "The Rock." Seen here with Bob Hill's stepdaughter on the front bumper, it made a great tow rig, even if there was no boat to tow. (Courtesy Bob Hill.)

Tow rigs came in all shapes and sizes. A few were bought special for the job, but most were rusty old clunkers. Some were held together with little more than Oregon Green twine and spray paint but still pulled the boat just fine. If it could haul a dory, it could be a tow rig. Mike Dixon used this 1976 Ford for many years. (Courtesy Mike and Kathy Dixon.)

Vic Learned Jr. constructed this dory in 1957 out of wood from his employer, Diamond Plywood in Tillamook. It was the first dory he ever built, and he named it the *Georgian*, after his daughter Georgiana. When enough people had mispronounced it, Learned rewrote the name as the *Georgi-Ann*. (Courtesy Terry and Jan Learned.)

Miss Kiawanda and the *Mossback* prepare to launch. This photograph is modern, but the dories are not. In the days before tilting trailers and access ramps, boats were left on the beach at the base of the cape. They were then either carried down to the water or rolled on logs or barrels. (Courtesy T. Larkins.)

A couple of inches of water was all that was needed to break the grip of the sand on the boat. Then, while one man waited in the dory, his partner would turn the boat around and push it into ever-deepening water, always mindful not to turn it sideways into breaking waves. (Courtesy T. Larkins.)

When the boat was deep enough and facing the right direction, the partner hopped in and assumed his set of oars. The two oarsmen then began the arduous task of rowing out through the surf. Moving in tandem, they powered through the waves and out to wherever they were fishing that day, sometimes as far as 12 miles north to Cape Lookout. (Courtesy T. Larkins.)

Steve Larkins stands at the console of his boat in 1973. As the dory evolved, new features were added, including a console to house the wiring for such items as CB radios and, later, fish finders and GPS units. The console also provided a mount for the steering wheel, air horn, and antennae and a place to stash lunch. (Courtesy T. Larkins.)

Early hand lines gave way to the quicker and more efficient hand-crank gurdies. Nowadays, gurdies are turned with hydraulics but maintain the same basic principle: a spool of wire weighted down and running to a given depth. Spreads are attached to the wire every 12 feet or so. (Courtesy T. Larkins.)

The pulley at the top of the gurdy pole operates the gurdy for the "tips," the lines that come off the commercial fishing poles that V upward out of a dory. The tips trail behind the boat as it trolls along. The pulley at the bottom operates the deep lines, which run off the sides of a dory. (Courtesy T. Larkins.)

In this more modern setup, the two spools sit side by side with the pulleys above them. The handle just to the right of lower center is turned to apply hydraulic pressure to the gurdies. The other handles are activated individually to control each gurdy.

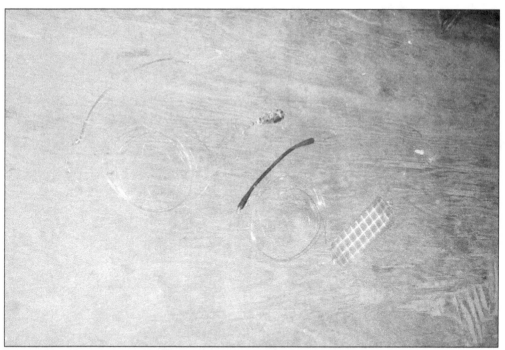

Pictured here are two spreads. A clip connects the whole spread to the gurdy line. Attached to the clip is a snubber, which helps keep the line from breaking. The leader is made of fishing line, and affixed to the end are any number of goodies attractive to fish.

This photograph shows a variety of commercial fishing gear. Fish are placed in the "kill box" after they are gutted. Stowed inside the box are the two floats that help support the long lines coming off the tips of the poles. In front is the cleaning tray, used to hold the fish while they are being dressed out.

In the early days, fish were laid out and gutted on the rocks at the base of Cape Kiwanda. Today that act would be illegal and would likely disturb the tourists, so it is not done. The gentleman standing on the right is Vic Learned Sr. Everyone else in the photograph is unidentified. The boat belonged to Keith Jones. (Courtesy Terry and Jan Learned.)

For the last 30 years at least, fish have been cleaned on the ocean. Ken Rosenbalm has a beautiful Chinook in the cleaning tray. The guts and gills are removed and thrown into the ocean, where they are immediately gobbled up by birds or other fish.

Jack and Marlene Hogevall owned the Kiwanda Fish Company for many years. Dorymen sold their catches to the fish company, which contracted with packing businesses to have the fish picked up and processed. Now fishermen must go hunting on their own for somewhere to sell their fish. Boats that used to bring in 175 fish a day are now sometimes lucky to catch 5. Fish companies could no longer turn a profit and were forced to abandon operations. One of the opinions voiced in 1927 was that coastal tourism is more profitable to the state than commercial fishing. While that opinion is debatable, the eventual decline of commercial fishing on the Oregon coast is unmistakable. Here Ken Rosenbalm off-loads a day's work from the *Jeanna L.* (Courtesy Mike and Kathy Dixon.)

Looking south from the sand dunes at the base of Cape Kiwanda, one can see tow rigs and trailers lining the beach. Dorymen remember the lines of trucks going two and three deep some days. Such is not the case anymore, and even when fishing was at its finest, very few people could turn it into a permanent living. (Courtesy Lloyd and Marilyn Rosenbalm.)

This view, looking north, shows the beach packed with a variety of tow rigs. There are army surplus vehicles, trucks of all shapes and sizes, and even a car or two. (Courtesy Lloyd and Marilyn Rosenbalm.)

The Oregon Department of Fish and Wildlife monitors the fish caught in the ocean waters off Pacific City. Even before the dory stops sliding, representatives are moving forward wanting to weigh and measure the catch. They check the size of the fish to make sure it is of legal length and scan the fish's nose for a metal tag. The tag reveals where the fish was put into the wild and helps track its movements. If the scan comes up positive for a tag, the gentleman or lady from fish and wildlife will simply cut off the nose and take it with them. These officials also ensure that a ventral or pectoral fin has been clipped. If so, the fish was hatchery raised and may be kept. If not, it must be thrown back. This is done in an effort to renew wild salmon runs.

Two

PACIFIC CITY AND CAPE KIWANDA

Pacific City and Cape Kiwanda have always been attractive to anglers. The Nestucca River, which winds through town and dumps into the ocean about a mile south of town, has had, for the most part, an abundant supply of salmon and Chinook. Local Native Americans took fish from the river but honored the salmon runs by observing the Law of the Pelican, which forbade catching salmon in bays or rivers until the migrating pelicans arrived in early July. This allowed a substantial amount of spawning salmon to make it upriver to lay their eggs, thus ensuring a bountiful crop of fish for the next year. With the relocation of local tribes to reservations, the fish had no one to catch them, and the salmon runs boomed. When people began settling the area anew, these pioneers found there was plenty to be had.

Farmers and dairymen supplemented their income with commercial fishing. When the Nestucca was closed to commercial fishing in 1927, the fishermen were forced to find some way around the law. They still had bills to pay. A few cast their nets in other nearby rivers, but these were not nearly as successful as the Nestucca. Some outlaws fished the Nestucca River at night, posting guards and creating diversions. Again, this was not as successful. Finally, they moved on to the waters of the Pacific. Boats could launch and land in the relatively calm waters in the shelter of the cape. The town of Pacific City already had a fishing industry, and Cape Kiwanda provided the means for it to continue. This chapter looks at a few of the landmarks in and around Pacific City and Cape Kiwanda.

This aerial view, taken in the late 1940s, shows just how sparsely populated Pacific City once was. The sandy areas on the left and lower portions of the photograph have absolutely no development. Today this area is crammed with homes, condominiums, townhouses, and the like, as is most of the town in the center. (Courtesy Oregon Department of Transportation.)

The natural protection provided by Cape Kiwanda, along with the sandy beaches, makes this a perfect place to host a dory fleet. The Nestucca River fishermen adapted their boats and equipment to the ocean and began again to bring in commercially caught salmon and Chinook.

Haystack Rock stands roughly a half-mile from the beach at Cape Kiwanda. Although it is off limits today, folks with the access and determination have gone out and climbed it. From this angle, the rock resembles a gorilla's head, as if the animal were looking toward the southwest. (Courtesy Bob Hill.)

This photograph was taken from an unidentified location. Anyone who has explored the cape and the tide pools at its base knows of the little cave along the wall, but it does not have a tree, nor is it this big. (Courtesy Tillamook County Pioneer Museum.)

The size and shape of Cape Kiwanda has changed tremendously over the years, as have the areas accessible to the public. Too many people have fallen to their deaths, especially on the north side, and therefore many sites are now restricted. The views from the remaining spots are amazing, though, and worth the effort of the climb. (Courtesy Tillamook County Pioneer Museum.)

People have enjoyed the ocean waters around Cape Kiwanda for decades. These folks appear to be involved in some sort of celebration or baptism. (Courtesy Tillamook County Pioneer Museum.)

Roseanne Goffena stops for a snapshot with baby Steve in her arm and little Leann beside her. They are standing on the dunes that form the backside of the beach at Cape Kiwanda. Down below is the 1960 Chevrolet convertible the family used as a tow rig for Stan Goffena's boat. Not too many convertibles pull boats these days—at least not any that come out of the factory as convertibles. Roseanne and the kids are probably enjoying a beautiful day at the beach while Dad is fishing. These dunes are now private access, designated only for owners of the nearby timeshare condominiums. (Courtesy Stan and Roseanne Goffena.)

Cape Lookout, as seen from Cape Kiwanda, lies roughly 12 miles north of Kiwanda. Note the spelling on the photograph as "Kiawanda"; Haystack Rock was reportedly called Chief Kiawanda Rock after a well-known Nestugga Indian chief. (Courtesy Tillamook County Pioneer Museum.)

This view, looking south toward Cape Kiwanda and Haystack Rock, was taken from an airplane somewhere over Cape Lookout. The line of sand in the trees is where the Three Capes Scenic Route runs today. Cascade Head can be seen in the upper portion, while the Nestucca River curves by on the left. (Courtesy Bob Hill.)

There is just something inherently beautiful about a coastline, whether it be Oregon's or any other state's. Above is another view looking south toward Cape Kiwanda from Cape Lookout. The distance is roughly 12 miles, but it seems to go on forever. Cascade Head is visible at the top of the photograph. At right is a closer view from the beach just north of Cape Kiwanda, but again looking south. Haystack Rock rises some 320 feet above the water and can be seen for miles around. The beach on the north side of the cape bears the same sandy texture that is so attractive to dory fishermen, but lacks the natural protection from the prevailing northwest winds provided by Cape Kiwanda. Sitting on the beach on the south side, one can feel a bit "tucked in," while the north is just wide-open sand. (Courtesy Oregon Department of Transportation.)

Despite the infrequency of the event (or perhaps because of it), there are many photographs of a snowy Haystack Rock. The two on this page take one's breath away with their simple and pure beauty. The pristine landscape in the foreground is the perfect frame for the magnificent image of Haystack Rock bathed in white. (Courtesy Bob Hill.)

Haystack Rock was initially called Chief Kiawanda Rock because it was said to resemble the head of a Native American chief. While the resemblance is hard to identify, an honor of that magnitude is not.

Water vapor rises from the ocean as the sun warms the chilly surface waters in this fabulous shot. T. Larkins says that the day that this was taken, everyone in the family went down to the beach and had a snowball fight. (Courtesy T. Larkins.)

Rob Kliever took this photograph just south of Cape Lookout. The view reveals the dorsal fin of an orca, or killer whale. Just to the right of the fin, just above the waterline, are the remnants of its spray. Dory fishermen bear witness—sometimes at very close range—to many critters inland dwellers only get to see in books and aquariums. Besides orcas and other types of whales, they have reported seeing dolphins, sharks, sea snakes, turtles, seals, sea lions, and ocean sunfish, which measure, on average, 6 feet long and weigh around one ton. This list is most likely short in comparison to what has actually been seen but unreported. It must be truly amazing to see these creatures up close and in their natural environment. (Courtesy Rob Kliever.)

Though the shoreline is protected just south of Cape Kiwanda, it still sees its fair share of destructive weather. It is the Oregon coast, after all. Coastal storms are impressive anywhere, and this little stretch of sand is no exception. In this photograph, taken from the parking lot at Cape Kiwanda in February 1999, a pile of debris blocks the access ramp to the beach. Sand and water have infiltrated the parking lot above the beach. Cape Kiwanda, shadowed in the background, has weathered many storms through the centuries, and although its shape has changed dramatically over the years, it endures as a testament to the volatility, perseverance, and strength of Mother Nature. (Courtesy Ken and Melva Rosenbalm.)

The beach at Cape Kiwanda is usually very clean and free of driftwood. Looking south along the beach from the base of the cape, this view reveals just how much damage was done in February 1999. The same storm that littered the beach at Cape Kiwanda with all of this debris littered the beach at Coos Bay with the freighter *New Carissa*. (Courtesy Ken and Melva Rosenbalm.)

It is no wonder the face of Cape Kiwanda has changed so much over the years. Nothing could take a beating like the one that hit this little sandstone hill and come out unscathed. In this February 1999 photograph, waves crash over the tip of the cape. While this is not unheard of, it is not necessarily common either. (Courtesy Ken and Melva Rosenbalm.)

Every once in a while, the coastal town of Pacific City gets some snow. Looking northeast through the only four-way stop in town, this view shows the Shell service station, which now looks very different. The tavern on the left remains. (Courtesy Bob Hill.)

This view, a little more due east, allows the station's three bay doors to be plainly seen. Also visible is an advertisement for the Dory Derby in August. (Courtesy Bob Hill.)

Haystack Rock provides a beautiful backdrop and must be one of the most photographed spots on the Oregon coast, even when compared with that *other* Haystack Rock up the beach a ways (Cannon Beach). The burg of Pacific City splays out in front of the beach, with the old hotel visible in the center. Someone's dory sits at the lower center. (One smart aleck noted that there must have been a pretty high tide to get the boat all the way up there.) Many dorymen live in Pacific City Heights, where this shot was taken. McMinnville Hill is a section where the folks from McMinnville seem to like to build their homes. Even though the view has changed a bit in recent years, the rock still stands solidly in the background. (Courtesy Bob Hill.)

Three

DORY CONSTRUCTION 101

A dory, by definition, is a flat-bottomed boat with two pointed (or nearly pointed) ends. The traditional dories of the Pacific City fleet were just that. Over the years, however, they have evolved into the square-stern variety seen today. Originally modeled after the Gloucester dory of New England, the Pacific City dory boat has come into its own. This chapter will take the reader through a series of photographs related to dory construction. When former Dayton High School basketball coach Earl McKinney wanted a dory built, he contacted Terry Learned of Learned's Boat Shop in Woods, Oregon. Most of the pictures in this chapter were taken during the construction of McKinney's *Rebounder*. Learned built his first boat when he was in high school and his first dory in 1967. He and his father, Vic Learned Jr., began constructing boats as a team in 1974. The boatbuilding tradition has been handed down to Terry Learned's daughters and granddaughter, as evidenced by the photographs of all four building the *Rebounder*, including daughter Annie, who was eight months pregnant at the time.

A small section at the end of the chapter discusses dory names. There are hundreds of names out there, and each one has a story. This author has chosen a handful to share but wanted to include so many more. An unbelievable amount of thought and creativity goes into naming one's boat. Some are named after family members, especially women, and others are just plain fun. Whatever the thought process, each boat is special. *Chief Kiwanda*, *Hunky Dory*, *A'Dory'O*, *Playin' Hooky*, *Hunk–A-Junk*, and *Hoochie Man* (a "hoochie" is a lure used to attract fish) are a few favorites.

Plywood comes in 8-foot-long sheets, and the average dory is just less than 24 feet long. Joining the 8-foot lengths into one continuous 24-foot span requires a technique called scarfing. Linking the boards with the lap joints tapered at a ratio of one to eight (1-inch-thick plywood to 8-inch-long scarf joint) will produce a joint that is comparable in strength to the rest of plywood. The scarfing machine is fairly new and can be a bit tricky but well worth the effort, as it produces a much cleaner scarf joint than older methods. This photograph actually hangs in the store in Spanish Fort, Alabama, where the John Henry model scarfing machine is sold and where Terry Learned purchased his. When customers complain about how difficult the machine is to use, the store patron simply points to the picture and says, "Well, out in Oregon the *girls* can use it." (Courtesy Terry and Jan Learned.)

Dory boats are built from ⅜-inch-thick marine-grade plywood. Using the one-to-eight formula, Terry Learned cuts a 3½-inch-long scarf joint. After the epoxy glue is applied, the second piece of plywood is rested against the first, clamped down, and allowed to cure for three or four days. (Courtesy Terry and Jan Learned.)

This view shows plywood that has been scarfed, clamped together, and left to cure. The cure time would be quicker but for the lack of heat in Terry Learned's shop. The sheets have been separated with wax paper and shims to prevent them from sticking. (Courtesy Terry and Jan Learned.)

All of the supplies are now in place: 24-foot lengths of ⅜-inch plywood, the bow stem, and 14 ribs assembled with two by sixes (although the ribs have not yet been notched out to allow for the keelsons, the longitudinal boards on the bottom of the boat). The only thing missing here is the transom. (Courtesy Terry and Jan Learned.)

Terry Learned's daughter Annie holds up the transom, which forms the aft section, or back of the boat. The transom for the *Rebounder* was built with ¾-inch-thick plywood and framed with old-growth Douglas fir. (Courtesy Charles Summers.)

Epoxy is applied to the bow stem, a piece about 5 feet long located at the very front of the boat. It serves as an attachment point for the sides of the dory. Terry Learned looks on as his daughter Annie spreads the epoxy. (Courtesy Charles Summers.)

Nailing the first side to the bow stem gets assembly off and running. The second side will soon follow. Once the sides have been attached to the bow stem, the boat will look something like a giant V until the transom is nailed into place. With the transom attached, the boat will then have a hull. (Courtesy Charles Summers.)

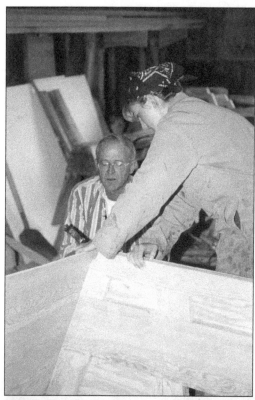

The transom is put into place, pulling the sides of the dory in. The definite shape of the dory comes later, with the installation of the ribs. Terry Learned hammers away as Annie supports the pieces. Epoxy has been applied anywhere wood meets wood, thus keeping out moisture and further strengthening the joints. (Courtesy Charles Summers.)

Two of the ribs are built around pieces of plywood. The first to be installed, these will form the front and back walls of the fish box. To hold the ribs in place while they are being nailed, a board is placed across the sides of the dory, and the ribs are attached to it with C-clamps. Learned says that after these two ribs are placed, the rest are a breeze. (Courtesy Charles Summers.)

About four hours into construction, all the ribs are in place. There are 14 sets of ribs spaced 15 inches apart in the average 22-foot dory. The notches on the underside of the ribs will house the keelsons, or "longitudinals," as Terry Learned calls them. With the ribs mounted, the dory now has a shape. (Courtesy Charles Summers.)

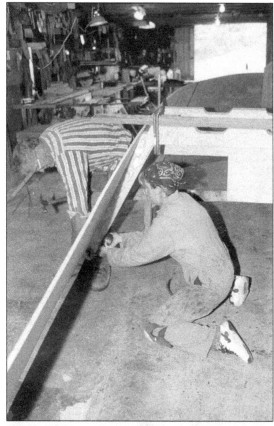

The ribs are installed, the hull shaped, and the keelsons bolted. Now it is time for the bottom. Lots of shaping and sanding will be involved to get the perfect fit. No daylight should show around the edges of the plywood. (Courtesy Terry and Jan Learned.)

Terry Learned claims his daughter Pam is always smiling and making the best of things. Here she stands in the little space between the ribs and the keelsons after spreading epoxy under the boat. Glue in her hair and all, she is still smiling. (Courtesy Terry and Jan Learned.)

With the plywood still in place, a pencil line is drawn along where it meets the forward hull. After the plywood is cut, it will be epoxied and nailed down to the bottom of the boat. The plywood on the bottom is butt-jointed together, not scarfed like the sides. (Courtesy Terry and Jan Learned.)

Following the pencil line that was drawn while the plywood rested tight on the upside-down dory, Terry Learned runs the circular saw along and cuts the piece. It will be butt-jointed with another piece of plywood to form the bottom of the boat. (Courtesy Terry and Jan Learned.)

The underside of the dory glistens in the light. Having been covered with epoxy, it now awaits the installment of the second bottom. (Courtesy Terry and Jan Learned.)

The bottom of a dory takes a heck of a beating each time it bounces through the surf or slides onto shore. For a sturdier boat, a second bottom has been shaped and cut and now waits to be put in place. The first bottom, seen in the background, has been slathered with epoxy. (Courtesy Terry and Jan Learned.)

Pam (left, foreground), Terry (center), and Annie Learned carry the larger of the two halves that will combine to make the second bottom of the boat. It has been shaped, measured, and cut just as the first bottom, and will be nailed down once in its proper place. (Courtesy Terry and Jan Learned.)

The ladies hold one piece of the second bottom while Terry Learned and his granddaughter Kami Learned bring in the other piece. Kami, around nine years old in this photograph, is Annie Learned's daughter. In 1996, Terry and Kami put together a dory by themselves. She was 13 years old. (Courtesy Terry and Jan Learned.)

The second, smaller piece is now in place and will be jointed against its mate. As opposed to the process of scarf jointing, the two pieces are simply butted together to make the seam. (Courtesy Terry and Jan Learned.)

Once the pieces of the second bottom are in place, the two bottoms are nailed together. Stainless-steel ring shanks, also called annular-ringed nails, are used for this job. This type of nail is not only resistant to corrosion, but adds to the life of the boat by biting into the wood. Terry Learned does not use any screws in the construction of his boats, as the screw's helical nature is not as secure as the annular rings on the stainless-steel nails. According to Learned, this job took about an hour to complete with the three of them steadily nailing. (Courtesy Terry and Jan Learned.)

Now it is time to flip the boat and perform finishing work to the main body. Terry Learned built this handy rack and then added two chain hoists to do the heavy lifting. At this point, the dory weighs approximately 900 pounds. He simply puts scooter boards (also built by Learned and seen in the foreground) in a few strategic locations and pushes the boat outside and into place, all by his lonesome. (Courtesy Terry and Jan Learned.)

Ken Rosenbalm's third boat, the *Jeanna L*, was built by Howard Kellow. Kellow kept exactly the same angle on each of his ribs, giving his boats a uniform shape. Learned boats, however, have a greater angle to the forward ribs, flaring the front out a bit. Learned explains that this pushes the water out more and helps the boat move through the ocean with greater ease. No two are alike. (Courtesy Charles Summers.)

This split view of the boat's interior shows the port side with the floorboard and the starboard without. The starboard keelson and half of the middle one are visible. The keelsons run the length of the boat and form its backbone. Dories are flat-bottomed boats, without a true keel, but they do have keelsons. (Courtesy Charles Summers.)

A side view from the left reveals the cover for the fish box in the lower left. The small door on the console allows access to the wiring for the CB radio, fish finder, and GPS and storage for smaller items. (Courtesy Charles Summers.)

Some dories include an opening for the fish box on both sides, but Terry Learned's boats have a pass-through on the right side, easing movement from the back of the boat to the front. The pass-through opens for more storage. (Courtesy Charles Summers.)

This photograph provides a close-up shot of the inside of the completed *Rebounder*. The fish trays are done, running along either side of the boat. The console has been placed, as well as both floorboards. All of the finishing work on the interior has been accomplished. (Courtesy Charles Summers.)

The notched-out area in the back is where the outboard engine will be mounted. Terry Learned says, "Nowadays the outboard-powered dories have the engine mounted right on the transom itself, rather than in a well, as they were for so many years. The lower unit cowling is so large on the modern, four-stroke engines, any well for the outboard would have to be huge to accommodate the steering capabilities, which would mean loss of flotation, and we don't want that." (Courtesy Charles Summers.)

His work done, Terry Learned stands with the completed *Rebounder* in front of his boatbuilding shop near Woods, Oregon. Learned built his first dory on the wood floor of his father's dairy barn in the fall of 1967. He was 27 years old and constructed the dory for himself. He named it *Sandgerdi*, after an Icelandic village he visited while in the U.S. Air Force. Terry Learned and his father, Vic Learned Jr., began building boats together in 1974. (Courtesy Charles Summers.)

Vic Learned Jr. was one of the original Pacific City fishermen. As a kid, he was paid with soda pop to stand guard over the contraband nets his father and uncles had placed in the Nestucca River. He is remembered as an amazingly kind man, full of knowledge and willing to share. His son Terry is a testament to that. Vic Learned Jr. died on August 11, 1998. (Courtesy Charles Summers.)

Terry Learned (left) stands with his father, Vic Learned Jr., at the stern of a 20-foot-long custom dory. Father and son began building dories together in 1974. Their first sold to Dave Schaeffer for $1,850. They now sell for $8,500. This photograph, taken 23 years later in 1997, shows them standing with the last boat they would construct as a team. (Courtesy Terry and Jan Learned.)

With plans and technical assistance provided by Terry Learned, Ken Rosenbalm started building this dory in 1992 and finished it in 1994. He began fishing with that boat that same year. Rosenbalm had been tossing around the idea of building a boat for many years. He had originally thought it would be fun to help another local boat builder, Jim Wharton, construct dories, but Jim did not want help, so Rosenbalm shelved that idea. When the means were finally available, Rosenbalm began building the *Warrior Pride*. It took two years, but he stuck with it and got it done. The final cost was around $30,000. He has already gathered up the pieces for his next dory. (Courtesy Ken and Melva Rosenbalm.)

In this shot, one can appreciate the length of the *Warrior Pride*. Built 4 feet longer than the average 22-foot dory, the *Warrior Pride* required an extra-long trailer to haul it around. This trailer was built by Lee Taylor, who gave it an additional set of tires for support. (Courtesy Ken and Melva Rosenbalm.)

Mike Dixon bought this boat around 1980 or 1981. Built by Jim Wharton, it was about four years old when Dixon purchased it from his friend. The whole family pitched in to get the *Hook-N-Eye* up to snuff and seaworthy. Dixon's son Alex is in the foreground. (Courtesy Mike and Kathy Dixon.)

Naming one's boat is serious business. The *Janet Ann* was named for a wife, as were many boats, but how about *Rebounder*, owned by former Dayton High School basketball coach Earl McKinney, or *Remedy*, owned by a pharmacist? There are the *Cod Father*, the *Cod Sucker*, and the *Happ-E Hook-R*. A whole slew of "Mama" boats dot the ocean, including *Mama's Competition*, *Mama's Mad*, *Mama's Money*, and *Mama's Worry*. A fleet of instrument-themed boats such as the *Fiddler*, *Mandolin*, *Banjo*, *Piccolo*, and *Guitar* could form a respectable band. The *Democrat* is a floating political message. Some boat names describe what their owners get, like *Numbutt*, *Soreback*, and *Deeper-N-Det*. Some tell how it is, such as *Where the Far-Car-We* and *Snafu*. The *Tuition* was given to two sons so they could earn money for college. The author will always prefer the dories named for daughters, like the *Georgi-Ann* and the *Jeanna L*. (Names compiled by Alice Learned; courtesy Mike and Kathy Dixon.)

Sometime before he acquired his dory, Rob Kliever was photographed duck hunting with a buddy. The image was published in a sporting magazine, but instead of Kliever, Rob was given the last name of Klevenger. Rob's good humor prevailed, and when he got his boat, he thought *Klevenger* would be a good name for it as well. (Courtesy Rob Kliever.)

Anyone who knows Ken Rosenbalm knows that he is the No. 1 fan of local high school sports. If not fishing, he can probably be found at a football, volleyball, or basketball game at Amity High School. The *Warrior Pride* is named in honor of those teams. (Courtesy Ken and Melva Rosenbalm.)

Greg Ostrum leans against Ken Rosenbalm's boat, the *Warrior Pride*, while Mike Dixon stands beside his own *Native Son*. Rosenbalm reports that he had intended to name his next boat *Native Son*. He had, in fact, told Dixon of his intentions and was none too happy with Dixon when he claimed it as his own. Rosenbalm has since gotten over it. (Courtesy Ken and Melva Rosenbalm.)

The *Native Son*, Mike Dixon's third boat, reflects beautifully on the glistening sand. Dixon purchased the Learned boat in 2002. Painted bright red and yellow with brown trim, it is impressive to see, both on the water and off. (Courtesy Ken and Melva Rosenbalm.)

Four

LAUNCHING AND LANDING

The unique design of the dory boat allows it to be launched from and landed on the beach. There are no moorings available in the little Nestucca Bay, as there are in others, so the dories do just that: they launch and land on the beach. Anyone who has visited the coast at Pacific City has probably seen—and been enchanted by—the spectacle. Running a dory in and out through the surf is fun but also dangerous; performing the maneuvers correctly requires strength and skill. Dorymen have long practiced their sport and have become experts at the required technique. They watch the ocean and know its signs. Perhaps more important, though, they respect the ocean and try not to do anything foolish. This chapter honors the skill of dory fishermen and explains a bit of what they do.

Before the introduction of square-stern dories and outboard motors for landing, dorymen did not have to worry too much about what was on the shore where they intended to land. They moved slowly enough that anything living would have time to move, and they avoided anything not living that might damage their boats. Now, with surfers, kayakers, and tourists jamming the beach, maneuvering can be a challenge. The beach at Cape Kiwanda is a commercial fishing port, and beach users must respect that. The old saying "Never turn your back on the ocean" applies to the dories as well. The boats are great fun to watch—but at a distance. More than one unknowing pedestrian has stood stalk still in the direct path of an incoming dory.

Taken at dawn, this view shows two boats headed out—one sport and one commercial. Haystack Rock looms large in the near distance and reflects beautifully in the sand. The sky is just beginning to lighten. One can imagine the early morning before this shot was taken. First, check the ocean and see if it is fishable. Next, stop for a quick coffee and maybe breakfast at the Sunset West Café. The atmosphere is jovial and light, peppered with curse words and seen through a haze of cigarette smoke. One last trip to the bathroom and then down to the beach. The bells on the tips of the poles tinkle as the men bounce down the ramp. Set out the poles, check the motor, turn on the CB radio, stash the cooler and any passengers on the boat, and all is ready. Back the boat into the surf and dump it, and race to the water after parking. Head out. (Courtesy Bob Hill.)

Sometimes the best thing to do is just hold on and pray. This impressive photograph illustrates one of the many inherent dangers of ocean fishing. The fish lie beyond the breakers, and sometimes getting through the waves to the fishing grounds can be a challenge. The dorymen must first push their way through the pounding—and unforgiving—surf. The sport of dory fishing requires agility, skill, and occasionally a bit of luck. Although there have been a few reported fatalities among dory fishermen, for the most part they have a good safety record. Boats have rolled over in the surf on occasion, but thankfully, there are only bumps, bruises, and broken bones to report. In an interview for the *Oregonian* newspaper, Howard Kellow put it clearly: "I've always had a big respect for that water. When she's too rough you just stay on the beach." These are wise words from a man who fished long enough to know. (Courtesy Ken and Melva Rosenbalm.)

It is daybreak on the Oregon coast, and the *Wendy Lou II* is ready to hit the water. Don White waits patiently, watching for a set of waves that looks good to him. When asked how he knows which are good, one experienced fisherman replied, "You just know. You've been doing it for so long, you just know." (Courtesy T. Larkins.)

Don White will continue to wait as he sees this breaker roll just in front of him. Dory boats are heavy, and the force of the waves is strong. Pushing against that force requires firm footing and a decent amount of strength. The water volume from the breaking wave will give the *Wendy Lou II* a tad more float. (Courtesy T. Larkins.)

The water is now up around Don White's knees and will get several inches deeper as this wave rolls on through. At that point, when the boat is deep enough that the motor will not drag in the sand and the going looks clear enough, White will hop in his boat, fire up the motor, and head on out. (Courtesy T. Larkins.)

The *Wendy Lou II* has just cleared the breakers and is on its way. It may have to slow down a few more times as it comes upon developing waves, but for the most part it is off and running. (Courtesy T. Larkins.)

This photograph may be another shot of the *Wendy Lou II*, but the angle just does not seem right. Breaking waves can be seen in the foreground as the boat heads toward Haystack Rock and then on to the fishing grounds. (Courtesy T. Larkins.)

The dory seems to disappear as it bobs in the water just offshore. The incoming swells are the next set of breaking waves on the beach, and their size determines that of the waves. A big set is typically followed by calmer water, and about every seventh wave is the biggest in the set. (Courtesy T. Larkins.)

Two unidentified dories race out for some sport fishing, as no commercial poles are erected on either side of the boats. They are headed southwest, below Haystack Rock, possibly to the waters off the mouth of the Nestucca River. (Courtesy T. Larkins.)

Sport fishermen hold on tight as they crash through an incoming wave. Cascade Head is visible to the left of the boat, along the horizon. (Courtesy Bob Hill.)

This dory, possibly named *Chance*, has made it through a fairly easy set. With Cape Kiwanda looming large in the background, it moves past the breakers. At this point, the motor is working fine, but note the oars leaning against the bow. (Courtesy T. Larkins.)

Should anything happen to the engine while on the water, the wayward fisherman can hopefully catch a tow from another boater, but not always. Even then, having been towed from wherever, he must still row through the surf on his own. Modern dory boats weigh about 3,000 pounds. (Courtesy T. Larkins.)

Stan Goffena and Willie Jones row through what looks to be fairly flat surf. With only one set of oars, they must turn and look at the incoming waves. This was typically done by the oarsman facing the open ocean. (Courtesy Stan and Roseanne Goffena.)

This photograph reveals that even nice, flat surf can give a little splash now and again. Stan Goffena and Willie Jones got a decent tilt off of this wave and possibly the one following it. (Courtesy Stan and Roseanne Goffena.)

Seagulls stand watch as this traditional double-ender waits for a little more lift. The dorymen of today avoid this area entirely. Speeding through the rocks would almost certainly cause a collision, and there is very little sand on which to slide. (Courtesy Bob Hill.)

In the following two photographs, Paul Hanneman (left, in the dark shirt) and his nephew (in the white shirt) row the new *Kiwanda Klipper 2* out through the toadstools. The boat bears the modern square stern and twin engines but is still being rowed through the surf to launch. (Courtesy Bob Hill.)

The boat prepares to move through two rocks, apparently a tight squeeze. The average dory is about 8 feet across at the draw, keeping it legal for towing down the road. Hanneman was a friend of photographer Bob Hill—and one of his favorite subjects. (Courtesy Bob Hill.)

Still showing Paul Hanneman and his nephew, this photograph was likely taken on a separate day from the first two, as the angle of the shot is different. Also, Hanneman's nephew is no longer wearing a shirt. Note the tilting of the boat and the water streaming from the underside. (Courtesy Bob Hill.)

Looking very closely at this 1983 image, at the back of the boat one can see Steve Macy hanging on as Paul Gilson guns it out through the surf. Apparently Macy was dragged through the waves a bit before getting into the boat. When asked what happened, Macy jovially replied, "No, that's how it always is. He does that all the time." Gilson and Macy have been friends since junior high school. They played football together growing up and now fish together as adults. The pair purchased their boat from Glen Macy, Gene Peterson, Kelt Peery, and Chuck Colvin. Christened by this group as the *Ridge Runner*, Gilson and the younger Macy renamed the boat *Ten-Thirty*, accusing the other group of sleeping in until that time of day. (Courtesy Steve Macy.)

The top of Haystack Rock is shrouded in fog as these three boats, including the *Klevenger* in the foreground, head out at dawn. With the possible exception of the *Ten-Thirty*, most dories launch at daybreak. (Courtesy Rob Kliever.)

The *Klevenger* crests a small wave as Rob Kliever starts out for the day. Launching on days like this does not seem so bad. It is cold and foggy, but the breakers are not too big and are spaced out nicely. The ocean beyond looks a little bit choppy. (Courtesy Rob Kliever.)

The *Six Pac* clears the top of a wave, the last in the series, and will soon enjoy smoother sailing. Once past the general area of the surf, dories usually have an easier time, though this is not always the case. (Courtesy T. Larkins.)

The *Six Pac* makes its way toward Haystack Rock and then beyond. At this point, just shy of the rock, the ocean waters are about 60 feet deep, or in nautical terms, 10 fathoms. (Courtesy T. Larkins.)

Steve Larkins runs in toward the beach. Dories typically stop about halfway between the rock and the beach to scan the surf and the shoreline for any obstacles—human or otherwise. (Courtesy T. Larkins.)

Finding a safe patch of surf and shore, Steve Larkins speeds up to motor through the waves. (Courtesy T. Larkins.)

The beach looks wide open as the *Jeanna L* returns. A dory rides the back of one wave while trying to keep ahead of the next. Then, as the wave breaks, the momentum pushes the dory in. (Courtesy Ken and Melva Rosenbalm.)

The breaking wave provides an added boost to the dory and shoves it up on the beach. When the bottom of the boat hits the wet sand, it slides along for a bit before stopping. Dory boats are sprayed with fiberglass so that they slide farther. Metal boats do not slide as well or as far as wooden ones. (Courtesy Ken and Melva Rosenbalm.)

The *Native Son* heads straight toward the toadstools while coming in for a landing, but modern dorymen steer clear of them. Earlier in the century, the calmest and deepest waters could be found around them, but not anymore. As Rosie Rosenbalm put it, "You have to have pretty hairy legs to get anywhere near them things these days." (Courtesy Mike and Kathy Dixon.)

As evidenced here, the *Native Son* has gone clear of the toadstools. Mike Dixon seems to have plenty of open water and unobstructed shoreline to land his boat. This must be a weekday because weekends see a dramatic rise in the population in and around Pacific City and Cape Kiwanda, resulting in a packed shoreline. (Courtesy Mike and Kathy Dixon.)

An unidentified boat motors into position for a smooth landing on the beach. The doryman will try to ride the building wave into shore. Slamming through the waves is very hard on a boat (not to mention its occupants) and should be avoided. (Courtesy T. Larkins.)

The *Jeanna L* seems to have a nice, clear beach, free of tourists and stray passersby, though what about the little black dot in the surf to the left of the boat? Is it a surfer, perhaps? The black dots behind the boat are other boats coming in, and off to the right, a buoy sticks up into the horizon. (Courtesy Ken and Melva Rosenbalm.)

With Cape Kiwanda standing watch in the background, the *Warrior Pride* sits patiently waiting for its trailer. The same natural protection and shore break that makes this spot so perfect for dory launching also makes it very attractive to folks wanting to spend a day at the beach. (Courtesy Ken and Melva Rosenbalm.)

The gentleman on the far right demonstrates where not to stand while watching the dories come in. How far a dory will slide once it hits the sand is anyone's guess. The best choice is to stand far back and out of the direct line. (Courtesy Rob Kliever.)

Dave Schlip hops from his boat to get his tow rig and trailer. He has probably stowed most of his gear and is ready to head back to wherever he parks his boat. The boat, trailer, and tow rig will have to be thoroughly hosed off before being put to bed for the night. Sand and salty seawater can do significant damage if left on the equipment. (Courtesy T. Larkins.)

The unique design of a dory trailer allows it to tilt upon hitting the bow stem of the dory. Then it rolls down and under the boat as the operator backs up. At a certain point, the trailer just starts pushing the boat along, and the operator has to stop, attach the winch, and crank the boat the rest of the way up. Modern winches are electric and therefore much easier on the arms. (Courtesy T. Larkins.)

Five

ON THE WATER

Over the years, ocean fishing has seen many changes. Fishing lines were originally hung off the boat and then pulled in hand over hand. After World War II, airplane gurdies were brought on board, transforming hand over hand into hand crank. When the idea came along to incorporate commercial outrigger poles, fishermen were able to increase the number of lines in the water but were still hand cranking those gurdies. Next to supply improvements was R. Barry Fisher, who figured out how to hook up a small hydraulic pump directly to the outboard motor. Hand cranking was no more. As discussed in other chapters, the actual boat has evolved as well, changing with the times.

Despite these improvements, dory fishing is still hard work—respectable hard work. Changes have made some parts of dory fishing easier, but certain things have remained the same: early mornings, long days on the water, and lots of waiting. The photographs in this chapter show some of what goes on during those long days afloat. Coffee gets drunk, cigarettes get smoked, and naps get taken. If one guy sleeps, the other watches constantly for that telltale jerking of the springs and listens for the tinkling of the bells. Early hardware is also displayed in this chapter.

Dory fishermen have hunted in packs from day one. For the most part, they let one another know where the fish are biting, so everyone usually heads in that direction. In the early years—and even today—the pack mentality ensured safety. Not originally equipped with radios, cell phones, and flare guns, boats were vulnerable on the open ocean. Whether they were rowing up to

Cape Lookout or fishing closer to home, the small handful of fishermen relied on each other for assistance, and they were actually able to handle many emergencies on their own. Cascade Head looms in the background as Ray Monroe (left), Scotty Fisher (center), and Ken Rosenbalm fish off the mouth of the Nestucca River. (Courtesy T. Larkins.)

Vic Learned Jr. scans the horizon from the bow of the *Georgi-Ann*. In the lower left and right are his first gurdies, spools with hand cranks attached to take the place of pulling lines hand over hand. (Courtesy Terry and Jan Learned.)

Seen here is the *Georgi-Ann*, with Terry Learned aft. Fresh from the U.S. Air Force in 1964, Learned fished the rest of the summer and married his wife, Jan, that fall. He says he was able to steer the motor with his feet from this seat. (Courtesy Terry and Jan Learned.)

Terry Learned's longtime friend Paul Hanneman took this photograph about 1955. The two are commercial fishing in the original *Kiwanda Klipper*, a double-ender owned by Hanneman. A commercial bow pole runs perpendicular across the boat, with the spring visible on the right, and the four oars rest on the bow as well. (Courtesy Terry and Jan Learned.)

Steve Larkins sits on his console, resting his left hand on the handle of the gurdy and his right hand just above the brake. This version of the gurdy is newer than in previous photographs. Hand cranking a gurdy required a significant amount of upper body strength and could obviously get very tiring. (Courtesy T. Larkins.)

Paul Hanneman checks the hand lines on the *Kiwanda Klipper*. Hand lines hung off of a galvanized steel spring attached to poles. The hand lines themselves consisted of woven cotton with a ⅛-inch diameter. Stainless steel would not be introduced until sometime in the 1960s. Bullet-shaped weights were placed every 12 to 18 feet, and the spreads were secured at these weights. Modern spreads are attached with clips and detached as each one surfaces. They are laid out in long trays on either side of the boat—neat and out of the way. These spreads were Oregon Green twine tied directly onto the woven cotton line. As the line was pulled up hand over hand, it was wound around a board. The weights and spreads had to be kept fairly organized. (Courtesy Terry and Jan Learned.)

Waiting for the next strike, Paul Hanneman sits back and takes a break. Terry Learned remembers that this spot at the back of the *Kiwanda Klipper* was a wonderfully comfortable seat. Haystack Rock, Cape Kiwanda, and Cape Lookout are visible in the background. The inboard motor sits in a well in the boat. During excursions in and out through the surf, these wells were plugged. The oarsman facing the ocean was usually standing right above the well and so got too wet without the plug. Once on the open water, the plug was removed and the motor inserted. Using an inboard motor to get through the surf was dangerous because it created too much tilt in a double-ender. (Courtesy Terry and Jan Learned.)

Dogs are the only animals susceptible to salmon poisoning. Not a true poisoning, salmon poisoning is actually caused by a microorganism called *Neorickettsia helminthoeca*, which infects a parasite called *Nanophyetus salmincola*, which then infects a salmon or any other anadromous fish (fish that swim upstream to spawn). To get this illness, a dog must have eaten an uncooked anadromous fish infected with the parasite infected with the microorganism. It sounds like a long shot, but it is fairly common and occurs with some regularity in this area. Signs of salmon poisoning include vomiting, diarrhea, fever, weakness, dehydration, loss of appetite, and swollen lymph nodes. Most folks are aware of the dangers of salmon ingestion and do not allow their dogs access to the fish. (Courtesy Terry and Jan Learned.)

If it is found in time, salmon poisoning is very treatable. After an antibiotic and a wormer, the dog will be as good as new. Left untreated, salmon poisoning is fatal in 90 percent of the canines that contract it. The 10 percent who are lucky enough to survive, however, will develop immunity and are free to chomp on salmon all they want. Cappy the cow dog was one of those blessed 10 percent. Not only did he develop immunity, but he acquired a particular taste for salmon. Specifically, he liked the gills. If there were fish to be dressed out and Cappy the cow dog was around, he got the gills. Owners Vic Learned Jr. and Terry Learned were undoubtedly happy to oblige. Feeding the gills to Cappy meant less mess for them to clean up. (Courtesy Terry and Jan Learned.)

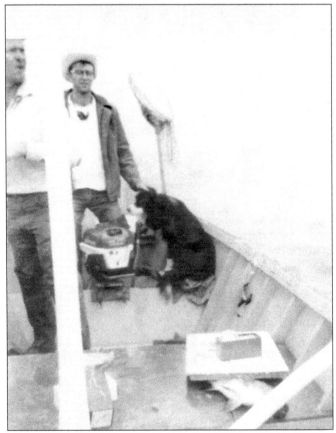

Steve Larkins hated searching for tuna, so he would start a rumor that they were out at some certain place and then everyone would head out there looking for them. He hoped that at some point the men would actually find the real location of the fish. But Larkins would get so excited when the rumors got back to him, he would chase out after his own imaginary tuna. (Courtesy T. Larkins.)

Getting comfortable for a nap on the boat is sometimes next to impossible. Dave Larkins takes uncomfortable to the extreme, though, by using the fish cleaning tray for a pillow. Fishing can be very hard work, and Dave was probably so tired it did not matter where he laid his head. (Courtesy T. Larkins.)

There is just something about the rocking of the boat and the slapping of waves on the hull that makes one want to take a nap. Or it could be the waking at the crack of dawn and the settling down after the initial rush of adrenaline that creates sleepiness. Whatever it is, with the boat swaying back and forth and the sun finally beaming down on one's numb little nose, a snooze is inevitable. It is a welcome respite from the boring part of fishing: the waiting. At least for this group it was. Layered with sweatshirts, coats, and life jackets and full with a morning snack, they could not help but fall asleep. Sierra Rosenbalm has the best seat on the boat—up on the warm motor cover. Little Ian Bottenberg is quite happy snuggled up with his older cousin Cody Rosenbalm. Fortunately, they woke up in time to catch a fish or two.

Fishing sometimes involves a lot of waiting, and these guys appear to be doing just that. One gentleman rests on the bench near the bow while the others stand in the back. The second man from the left appears to be setting his pole into the holder anchored to the side of the boat. (Courtesy T. Larkins.)

This photograph provides another view of our four friends waiting as the fish play hide and seek. The striking part of this photograph is how perfectly flat the ocean seems—as smooth as glass. (Courtesy T. Larkins.)

Even though the boat looks like it is sinking into the swell, it really has only dropped a few feet. It is time to head in when the other boats on the ocean are disappearing completely and the only thing seen from the trough between swells is the sky above. (Courtesy T. Larkins.)

The *Minga* trolls the waters just off of Neskowin. Lloyd "Rosie" Rosenbalm named his boat after his wife, Marilyn, which was too hard for the grandkids to say, so they called her Minga. The nickname stuck. (Courtesy T. Larkins.)

Rosie Rosenbalm floats close to a crab pot, the natural enemy of the dory fisherman. A tangle with a crab pot is not pretty and can ruin an otherwise beautiful day. Spreads, leaders, flashers, bait, weights, floats, and all the other paraphernalia of commercial dory fishing are expensive to replace, as are crab pots. (Courtesy T. Larkins.)

With Neskowin behind him, Rosie Rosenbalm relays a message on his CB radio. Rosenbalm remembers that he was logging near Neskowin and could hear the fishermen on the CB in his truck. Having a hard time staying focused on the trees, he was grateful when his day was done and he could go fishing. (Courtesy T. Larkins.)

This next series of photographs features the *Outlaw*, owned by Al Jensen. Like the guys we saw earlier in this chapter, the gentlemen on this boat seem to be playing the waiting game. (Courtesy T. Larkins.)

The men are jovial enough, though, and take a break from their coffee to wave a friendly hello. Members of the fishing brotherhood recognized this boat immediately because of the three gurdies and the "great big console." (Courtesy T. Larkins.)

It is the moment any fisherman lives for: when a fish takes the bait and runs. While the lucky pole owner plays his fish, the driver makes sure the boat does not turn and tangle the lines. (Courtesy T. Larkins.)

Now the net comes out. Some definite skill is involved in getting the net around the fish. The fish always seem to be kicking and fussing when one tries to bring them in, and getting in a tangle is pretty easy. (Courtesy T. Larkins.)

The tensest part of fishing seems to be coercing the fish into the net. Once that is done, the fisherman is pretty much home free—unless, of course, the fish is not a legal catch. While the fish is being played, it could still get away, but in the net, it is as good as in the bag. (Courtesy T. Larkins.)

The guys on the *Outlaw* have landed their fish and are now admiring the catch. Once the hook is removed from the mouth and the fish determined to be legal, it will be placed in the fish box. Tiny holes on the sides of the box allow a bit of ocean water in as well, to keep the fish fresh. (Courtesy T. Larkins.)

Ray Monroe works at gutting his fish in the tray. Some guys clean their fish on the motor cover, and others have cleaning trays that mount in a special spot. It is all a matter of preference. (Courtesy T. Larkins.)

Plenty of birds circle around at fish-cleaning time. They know a good snack when they see it and are not shy about letting fishermen know they are hungry. A goodly amount of the time, the remnants that are tossed do not even hit the water. The gulls just snatch them out of the air. (Courtesy T. Larkins.)

Ray Monroe dips his cleaned fish into the ocean water for a final rinse. The two seabirds on the right are hoping he drops it. (Courtesy T. Larkins.)

Monroe knows he has been spotted. He shows his appreciation at being photographed by giving the one-fingered wave. Or maybe he is relaying how many fish he caught or pointing to a particularly interesting cloud. (Courtesy T. Larkins.)

Ken Rosenbalm bought his first dory in 1975 and has been fishing the ocean waters ever since. This classic photograph shows Rosenbalm in his third boat, the *Jeanna L*, floating peacefully in the waters of the Pacific Ocean. As Rosenbalm would say, the ocean was "flatter than a fritter." He joined the dory fleet during its heyday in the 1970s. It has not always been easy or fun, and it has certainly caused more than one fight with his wife, but the memories go on and on. Dory fishing gets into your soul and becomes a part of who you are. (Courtesy T. Larkins.)

Six

THE CATCH

It does not get much better than this. One of the perks of fishing is getting to show off the catch. This chapter is dedicated to that very thing: showing off. Fishermen should hold their fish high and smile because they have earned it. A lot of waiting is involved in fishing, and many days the fisherman comes home with nothing to show for all this waiting except maybe a touch of frostbite. He gets up early, drives for hours, and then climbs up hills and down banks to get to his favorite spot. He stands for what seems like forever in the freezing cold only to be denied the one thing he is after.

This chapter celebrates those days when all the stars are in alignment, when the fishing gods are smiling down, the fisherman has worn his lucky hat, or that new hoochie has worked.

This photograph was titled "One hour's catch at Pacific City." Reports from the beginning of the century tell of boats bringing in three and four loads of fish a day. If a fisherman was lucky enough to find the school, he could have plenty. That was on the Nestucca River, but bottom fish, as these seem to be, have always been plentiful around Haystack Rock, and there is little doubt that this caption holds true. The reef that houses these delicacies runs from Haystack Rock up to the north end of Tierra del Mar and out to approximately 20 fathoms, or 120 feet deep. (Courtesy Tillamook County Pioneer Museum.)

Two unidentified gentlemen look on as Vic Learned Jr. (left) probably points out the fish he will add to the pile already on the beach. These days spectators often approach the boats after they have landed, hoping to catch a glimpse of the day's catch; apparently 50 years ago they did the same. Most fishermen are more than willing to show off their quarry. Just look at the walls of any sporting goods or fishing store to see countless photographs of men, women, and children holding up a gleaming fish or two. (Courtesy Terry and Jan Learned.)

Roseanne Goffena stops for a shot with her catch on a foggy day sometime in 1964. It looks to be one salmon and one Chinook. (Courtesy Stan and Roseanne Goffena.)

Posing with his halibut in 1963 is Stan Goffena. He remembers this one weighing in at around 50 pounds. Despite a tendency toward seasickness in his later years, Goffena continues to fish the waters off Cape Kiwanda, just as he has for more than 50 years. (Courtesy Stan and Roseanne Goffena.)

A small gathering of onlookers admires the mess of fish being cleaned by Paul Hanneman. As per custom, the fish are laid out and gutted on the rocks at the base of Cape Kiwanda. This makes for a great spectator sport, with seagulls waiting just out of the shot for a bit of the leftovers. Something primitive must not have evolved out of humans, because plenty of folks are always willing to watch the presentation of the kill. And while fishing has become more sport than necessity, there are still those who would eat fish every day if their family would allow them. (Courtesy Terry and Jan Learned.)

Gary Hill (left), Rob Kliever (center), and Warren Lamb have limited out this day in the mid-1980s. It has been a good day when everyone on the boat catches his limit. Kliever's son Alex stands with his dad, safely out of the drip zone. (Courtesy Rob Kliever.)

Hank Kliever holds up what looks to be a pretty good sized salmon. This photograph was taken on the ocean sometime between 1976 and 1978. (Courtesy Rob Kliever.)

Ken Rosenbalm keeps a cheap camera in his truck and takes it with him on any fishing trip, whether it is to ocean, river, pond, or puddle. The walls of his barbershop are covered with smiling folks holding up their catch. Rosenbalm is usually more interested in making sure everyone else catches a fish than he is about catching one himself, but every once in a while he gets to pose for a shot of his own. In the above photograph, taken in July 2002, he shows off two beautiful Chinook. At left, with Haystack Rock off his right shoulder, Rosenbalm has four silvers strung on his gaff hook. Rosenbalm does not necessarily fish to eat; he fishes because he loves it, and he also loves to share the fish he has caught. It is not unusual for him to show up at a neighbor's door with a fresh catch or some smoked salmon. All of his fish are smoked by longtime friend Dave Robertson Jr. (Courtesy Ken and Melva Rosenbalm.)

In 1980, schools of bait were sitting on the north side of Cape Kiwanda. Needless to say, schools of bait attract schools of salmon and Chinook looking for dinner. Rob Kliever remembers boats backed in, lined up in rows, and catching fish hand over fist. Pictured from left to right are Warren Lamb, Sterling Trowbridge, Brad Foster, David Brinker, Mark Irich, Rob Kliever, Ron Harland, and Joanne Harland. The gunther fish in the middle of the pack weighed in at 32 pounds dressed out. (Courtesy Rob Kliever.)

Steve Larkins looks pretty smug as he poses for this photograph. He should be; just holding up that monster with one hand is a proud moment. Larkins is getting ready to drop this beautiful Chinook into the fish company's scales below. Craig Wenrick now has one of those scales hanging in his shop. T. Larkins once said that she did not think there was anything sexier than a fisherman with his hip boots folded down below her knees. One night, she answered a knock on her door to find Steve in all his glory, with nothing on but a smile and his hip boots, folded down below his bare knees. (Courtesy T. Larkins.)

Cody Rosenbalm knows the rules for proper fish photographing: just stick your hand in there, hold up the fish, and smile. His little sister Tyra was not as easy to convince. Catching her first fish on her grandpa Ken's boat was really cool, but holding the fish for the traditional photograph was a different story. Putting her hand in a dead fish had a yuck factor of 10, and she opted for the less icky route. (Courtesy Ken and Melva Rosenbalm.)

Dustin Johnson, however, has no problem sticking his hand in there but is not quite able to lift the monster he brought home on this day in 1991. Johnson is all grown up now—and quite able to hold a fish. Grandpa Rosie Rosenbalm finds another fish in the boat and buddy Leo Godsey (left) lends a hand. Rosenbalm thinks this may have been Johnson's first ocean-caught salmon. (Courtesy Lloyd and Marilyn Rosenbalm.)

Young Cy Rosenbalm is all smiles as he hefts this one up for a snapshot. Lending a supportive hand is grandpa Ken Rosenbalm on the *Warrior Pride*. Fishing with grandpa is always a treat, and this day in the late 1990s was no exception. Note the telling statement on Ken's hat—his philosophy in a nutshell.

It has been a good day on the water when the fish caught is bigger than the cooler to carry it home. This may actually be the snack cooler, but it is still an impressive fish. This 13-pound silver was caught by Rob Kliever in the late 1970s. (Courtesy Rob Kliever.)

It is not unusual for big fish to eat little fish. It is the natural order of things. Big fish also find that little fish caught on a hook are fairly easy prey. That is what happened here. Big fish tried to eat little fish, but big fish got snatched into the boat instead. Rob Kliever hooked the little guy on the right and was reeling him in. Apparently, the bigger cod on the left also wanted that fish, because just as Kliever was getting ready to net the little one, the big one showed up, looking to snack on his fallen comrade. Kliever was quick enough to get the net around both fish, quite neatly scoring two for the price of one. He stands here beaming with his catch. (Courtesy Rob Kliever.)

Cousins Cody Rosenbalm (left), Ian Bottenberg (center), and Sierra Rosenbalm love going out on their grandpa Ken's boat. Part of the excitement is getting to "run" from one point to the next. On this day in July 2007, Sierra was the only one lucky enough to catch a salmon, so the *Warrior Pride* headed in toward Haystack Rock, where the bottom fish are plentiful and opportunity abounds. Cody just wanted to catch fish, but even he might admit that nothing beats the thrill of running across the ocean, feeling the wind and tasting the salt as bits of spray hit one's face. This intimacy with the ocean is part of the allure of dory fishing. It is better than any video game these children could ever have. Judging by the faces in the below photograph, their day is living up to expectations. All of the grandkids love fishing with grandpa.

This beautiful 15-pound Chinook was Sierra Rosenbalm's first fish. She had just asked how she would know if she caught a fish when this one hit. Her aunt Jeanna explained to her that she needed to watch the tip of her pole. If there was a fish, it would start jerking around. She had to hastily add "just like that" to the end of the sentence because the fish chose that very moment to strike. It is funny how everyone seems to remember his or her first fish, like a first kiss or a first date.

Seven

CELEBRATING THE DORY

Pacific City had long played host to an annual Fly In Fish Fry, but the popular event became too large to continue. In 1959, committee members Connie Wright, Jack Llewellyn, Harvey Henderson, and Dutch Shermer, as well as chairman of the committee Paul Hanneman, sought to replace the Fish Fry with something more manageable and something that would celebrate the tradition of dory fishing in the area. They came up with the Dory Derby, which debuted on August 30, 1959. The participants in the first Dory Derby all wore derby hats and competed in such events as rowing, racing, skin diving, and even waterskiing on the surf, with the skiers pulled by Jeeps driving along the shore.

The Dory Derby lives on today as the Dory Days, which continue to celebrate dory fishing in the community with a parade, rowing races, speed races, vendor booths, and of course a fish fry. Rain or shine, the event goes on—although shine is much preferred. That first Dory Derby was nearly fogged out, and the most recent was held over two days of wet weather varying between a drizzle and steady rain. Many different prizes have been offered to those taking the top honors, including a dune buggy, a 40-horsepower motor, and a new dory. Competition is always friendly and fun. The fish fry has been reported as possibly the best around.

Honoring the traditions laid out by the original dory fishermen is important to the community of Pacific City, as well as the members of the Pacific City Dorymen's Association. The Dory Days are one way to keep those traditions alive.

Photo by Bob Hill
Pacific City

Looking south from the top of Cape Kiwanda, this view shows the unbelievable amount of people drawn by the excitement of the Dory Derby. The stretch of beach, roughly a half-mile long, is just crammed with cars, trucks, boats, trailers, and people. This photograph also offers evidence of how the sand dunes (upper right) looked before hundreds of homes began crowding the area. It seems every square inch is being used up by civilization, and more and more homes are being built every day. The hill on the far right will soon host a new housing development, and condominiums have moved in just to the left of the access ramp. (Courtesy Bob Hill.)

121

This aerial view, looking north toward the cape, reveals that 10 years after starting, the Dory Derby is still going strong. Participants and spectators fill the beach. This shot was taken in the late 1960s or early 1970s, according to the photographer. It would be interesting to know how many of the recreational vehicles pictured ended up stuck in that sand. (Courtesy Walt Miller.)

Sandy Hanneman waves cheerfully from atop this dune buggy in a 1960s promotional photograph for the Pacific City Dory Derby. Her companion in the driver's seat is unidentified. Sandy's husband, Paul Hanneman, was one of the original organizers of the popular event. It lives on today as the Dory Days. (Courtesy Bob Hill.)

One of the highlights of the Dory Derby—or Dory Days, as it is now called—is the parade. Paul and Wanda Hill, owners for many years of the Shell gas station in downtown Pacific City, served as grand marshals the year this picture was taken. They are seen in a mid-1920s Chevrolet. Paul and Wanda moved their family from Gleneden Beach, Oregon, to Pacific City during the summer of 1962. (Courtesy Bob Hill.)

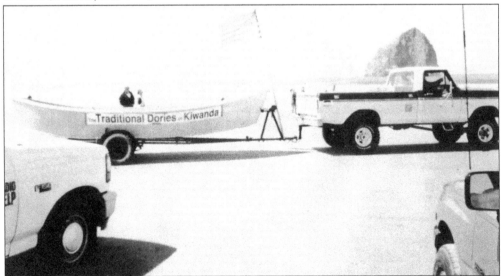

Each year, the parade features the traditional dories of Cape Kiwanda. This one, photographed in 1998, happens to belong to Dennis Brutke and is seen here on the beach before heading out to the water. Brutke aptly named his green boat the *Pea-Pod*. (Courtesy Daryn and Janell Brutke.)

At the first Dory Derby in 1959, the participants each wore a derby hat, as shown here. The boat on the left belonged to Roger Anderson. In this first race, the participants had to row out and around Haystack Rock and back to shore. As one contestant put it, "Rowing that far, that hard, nearly killed us," so that particular route was not used again. Ed and Bill Sears took top honors. (Courtesy Alice Learned.)

That first Dory Derby also featured a skin-diving contest. Members of the Salem Aqua Lungs had one hour to spear the biggest fish. Participants reported seeing a shark and two large whales while searching out their quarry. Laverne Fergusson of Netarts won this competition. (Courtesy Alice Learned.)

Various prizes have been offered through the years, including a dory. In May 1967, it was a dune buggy. This photograph was taken in front of the Shell service station owned by Paul and Wanda Hill. In the upper right corner, a sign advertises the Dory Derby. (Courtesy Bob Hill.)

Stan Goffena (left) and Dennis Brutke competed in the rowing race for about 10 years, Goffena thinks, beginning that first year, 1959. This mess of trophies was acquired one year, with Goffena and Brutke taking the top spot. The prize was a 40-horsepower engine, which they sold to a cousin and split the money. (Courtesy Genevieve Brutke.)

BIBLIOGRAPHY

"Dory Fishermen Struggle to Survive." *Tillamook PUD*. April 2002.

"For the Love of It." *Pacific Northwest Quarterly*. January or February 1991.

Gardner, John. *The Dory Book*. Camden, ME: International Marine Publishing Company, 1978.

Headlight-Herald. Tillamook, OR. 1959, 1978, 1981, 1998.

home.comcast.net/~dorypage

Larkins interview. 2007.

Learned interview. 2007.

Oregonian. Portland, OR. 1970, 1973, 1977.

"Pacific City Dories." *Oregon Coast*. July/August 1994.

"Yankee Ingenuity Helps Oregon Dory Fishermen with a Useful Hydraulic System for Outboards." *National Fisherman*. October 1970.

INDEX

Visit us at
arcadiapublishing.com

CPSIA information can be obtained
at www.ICGtesting.com
Printed in the USA
LVHW061248070723
751706LV00009B/850